D1275940

MARSHALL COUNTY PUBLIC LIBRARY
@ CALVERT CITY
23 PARK RD. P.O. BOX 465
CALVERT CITY, KY 42029

B-17

FLORISTS' REVIEW

FLOWERS FOR THE TABLE

Creating the perfect table with flowers and style

Designs by Talmage McLaurin, AIFD

Colombia.
Land of Flowers

Colombian *grown*

THE FINEST QUALITY CUT FLOWERS IN THE WORLD

FlorVerde

Good for the earth
for the workers
for you

www.florverde.org

The extraordinary flowers that fill the pages of *Flowers for the Table* were grown in Colombia, which is the largest supplier of fresh flowers to the United States and the second largest exporter of cut flowers in the world.

Colombia's flower industry, just over 40 years old and generating more than 225,000 legitimate direct and indirect jobs, is a shining example of responsible floriculture, supplying a global role model of economic, social and environmental initiatives. Due in great part to the influence of Florverde®, Colombian floriculture's socio-environmental standard and certification label, more than 700 million stems of responsibly grown flowers leave Colombia each year to enhance the lives of flower lovers around the world.

Colombia's advantageous geography supplies optimum year-round conditions for flower farming. Reliable sunlight, high altitude, fertile soil and abundant water provide the most perfect environment in the world for growing flowers, but it's the commitment and passion of the Colombian people that have made Colombia, truly, the land of flowers.

Colombia
Land of Flowers

Talmage McLaurin, AIFD, whose designs fill the pages of this book, is the publisher of *Florists' Review Enterprises*, the floral industry's oldest and only independent publishing house. He has been with the company since 1990. His floral career began in a family-owned flower business.

Talmage is a member of the American Institute of Floral Designers (AIFD); he was inducted in 1988. He has made five presentations to the institute at National Symposiums, and in 2003 he co-chaired the National Symposium, "The Prairie School." In 2008, Talmage received the AIFD award of Distinguished Service to the Floral Industry.

Talmage's column and designs appear regularly in *Florists' Review* magazine. His work is also featured in a number of books from Florists' Review, including *Wedding Bouquets* (2010), *Ribbons and Flowers* (2008), *101 How-To Favorites Volume 2* (2007), *Flower Arranging* (2007), *101 Great Displays* (2005), *Christmas Traditions* (2004), *Weddings 2* (2004), *Design School* (2003), *101 Wedding Bouquets* (2002), *Seasons of Flowers* (2001), *101 How-To Favorites* (2000), *World Floral Artists 2* (1999), *Weddings* (1998), and *Christmas* (1996).

CONTENTS

SPRING FLING

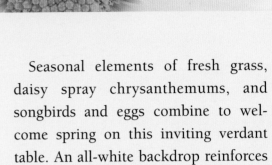

Seasonal elements of fresh grass, daisy spray chrysanthemums, and songbirds and eggs combine to welcome spring on this inviting verdant table. An all-white backdrop reinforces the simplicity and focuses attention on the early-spring hues.

Square, clear plastic containers covered in variegated lily grass (*Liriope*) form organic vessels for the daisies, and affordable glass bird votive holders become tiny bud vases and potential party favors. The remaining snips of lily grass are cut into even lengths and laid in loose groupings atop the napkins. As guests set the blades aside, the clippings will remain on the table to keep the fresh-cut aesthetic.

A pair of cubical clear plastic containers filled with faux robin's eggs serve as "bookends" to the row of grass-enveloped daisies and add another hint of color.

GRASS CONTAINERS

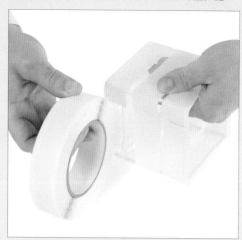

Apply three strips of double-sided adhesive around the sides of a square plastic container, encircling the bottom, middle and top of the cube. Remove the paper backing to expose the adhesive.

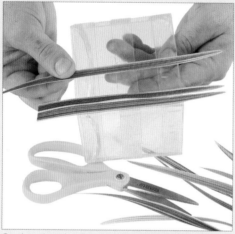

Cut lengths of variegated lily grass (*Liriope*) several inches longer than the container height, and press the blades to the adhesive. Make sure the tops of the grass blades line up and that the sides of the cubical container are entirely covered.

Trim the bottoms of the grass blades even with the base of the container. Working on one side of the container at a time allows for easier trimming, rather than waiting until all four sides are covered with lily grass.

WATER SOURCE

Place the square grass-covered containers into shallow trays filled with flower-food solution, to hydrate and keep the grass fresh. If multiple trays aren't available, a single rectangular platter could be used.

Fresh grass serves dual roles in this spring-green setting.

Spread the love with a quartet of heart-shaped flower boxes – crafted from cake pans – and chenille hearts. Lavender-hued 'Cool Water' roses ring the table in modern bud vases, and vintage 1950s valentines set the clever, kitschy tone.

Salal leaves camouflage the cake pans, which are filled with floral foam, and leaf-covered wood hearts edged with chenille stems suggest the flower boxes' lids. Spray adhesive holds the leaves in place.

Pink and red *Gerberas* join the 'Cool Water' roses and 'Nikita' spray roses in the lush mounds, with a few touches of statice and *Hypericum* sprinkled in. Red gumdrops set off the heart motif in the dishes and saucers.

The cheerful table will delight any group of guests, from couples celebrating romance to good friends toasting close ties.

CHENILLE HEARTS

Cover a papier-mâché heart ornament with spray adhesive. Apply red chenille stems on the diagonal, placing them side by side to cover the heart. Trim the chenille stems so they follow the heart's outline. Repeat on the reverse side.

To cover the side, gather three chenille stems side by side and push them into the heart at its cusp. Apply a bead of glue around one side of the heart, and wrap the stems onto it. Trim the ends at the heart's base.

Repeat Step 2 on the opposite side of the heart. Where the chenille stems meet at the heart's base, trim them to fit, and apply hot glue to secure them together.

HEART-SHAPE TRAYS

Spray the sides of a heart-shaped metal cake pan and the backs of the salal leaves with spray adhesive. Apply salal leaves in an overlapping horizontal pattern to cover the sides of the pan.

Instead of boxed chocolate, serve up flowered hearts.

Go all green when gathering friends and family to celebrate St. Patrick's Day, and add a liberal dose of the iconic shamrock. This fun table setting proves that a monochromatic color scheme is anything but boring when a variety of like hues are incorporated.

Clever oversized shamrocks crafted of *Galax* leaves spring from beds of naturally green carnations. Using a foam brush and acrylic paints, color each side of the square ceramic containers a different hue, from lime to emerald. The same paints color the miniature clay pots, each of which holds a *Galax* shamrock in a bit of floral foam covered with reindeer moss. Rectangles of green vellum form the napkin pockets, each topped with a single shamrock.

Guests will be ready to raise their glasses for a toast of "Erin Go Bragh!"

GALAX SHAMROCKS

Download a sheet of shamrock leaf patterns at *www.floristsreview.com/flowersforthetable*, and print the sheets in color.

Loosely cut out the paper shamrock leaves, and affix them to the backsides of *Galax* leaves with spray adhesive. Position each paper shamrock leaf so that its nonexistent stem would align with the *Galax* leaf stem.

Cut the *Galax* leaves into faux shamrock leaves by trimming around each paper shamrock pattern. Leave the paper patterns on the backs of the *Galax* leaves to add weight, body and different color and texture to the leaves.

VELLUM NAPKIN POCKETS

Fold in the sides of a rectangle of vellum so that they overlap, and tape them down. Fold the bottom up, and tape it. Turn the pocket over, and insert a napkin.

Varied grades of green provide St. Patty's day pop.

16

EASTER PARADE

For a whimsical take on a classic Easter pairing, this table offers a flock of sassy puffball chicks surrounded by a wealth of chocolate eggs. The brown-centered daisy spray chrysanthemums clustered in the main arrangement inspire the sunny yellow and chocolate brown hues, an alternative to traditional Easter pastels.

Faux eggs are sprayed glossy brown – giving the illusion of solid chocolate – and set into miniature white-painted flower pots or nestled into handfuls of bear grass clippings. The same paint can turn baskets or bunnies into similar "chocolate" creations, if desired.

Stealing the show are the cheery handmade chicks whose varied stances showcase loads of personality. And glasses filled with malted milk balls and tied with ribbon ensure everyone leaves with a sweet treat.

FUZZY CHICKS

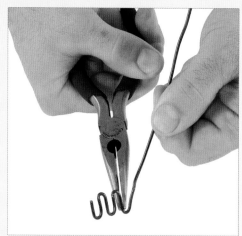

Cut a length of brown metallic wire. Using needle-nose pliers, bend sharp turns into one end of the wire to create three toes. Repeat at the other end of the wire.

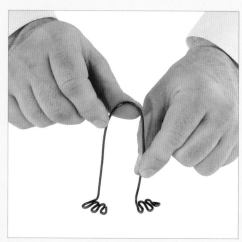

Bend the wire in an arch shape, and bend and shape the feet so that they stand flat to support the chick. Be creative with the chicks' stances, to give each a bit of attitude.

Knot a yellow marabou feather boa around the center arch in the wire. Continue tying additional knots until the pouf is the desired size. Trim the ends of the boa, and fluff.

CHOCOLATE EGGS

Impale each faux egg onto a heavy-gauge wire, inserting the other end of the wire into a foam block. Spray the egg with October Brown floral spray. Let dry, and remove the wire.

Turn anything "chocolate" with a coat of glossy paint.

MARSHALL COUNTY PUBLIC LIBRARY
@ CALVERT CITY
23 PARK RD. P.O. BOX 465
CALVERT CITY, KY 42029

21

BOOKS AND BLOOMS

Treasured texts and delightful details are sure to spark discussion among a book club or other literary group.

Peach spray roses, feathery 'Green Trick' *Dianthuses* and a few green salal leaves pop against the muted duotone backdrop, which features old pages recycled into striking leaf covers. Dust jackets folded from rectangles of kraft paper surround modern titles to blend with and round out the collection of antique books. Kraft paper boxes, lined with plastic, hold the bouquets. And medicine-bottle bud vases and carved bone finger bowls add a touch of sheen.

The stylish library lamps are crafted from silver candlesticks. Paper shades top white taper candles that are cut short. They can't be lit, but the overall effect is impressive, solidifying the bookish theme.

TEXT-TOPPED LEAVES

Spray the fronts of salal leaves with adhesive. Allow a few moments for the adhesive to become tacky, about 30 to 45 seconds.

Press the leaves onto a yellowed page from an old book. The pages can be taken from damaged texts, or look for bundles of pages in antique shops.

Cut around the leaves. On the multileaf stems of salal, keep some of the green leaves unadorned, for variety.

LEAK-PROOF LINERS

To create a liner for the kraft paper box, fold down the top of a zippered plastic bag, and place a square of floral foam inside. Press the bag and foam into the box.

A few green leaves contrast the text-covered foliage.

A collection of traditional glazed American pottery is the inspiration for this palette of pleasing pastels to honor Mom and, perhaps, showcase some of her favorite vintage pieces.

Fragrant garden roses – 'Caramel Antike', 'O'Hara', 'Alabaster' and 'Mariatheresia' – *Freesias* and Queen Anne's lace make elegant adornments for the winged vases and their smaller counterparts at each place setting.

The large mat of inexpensive acetate ribbons woven into a customized plaid creates a colorful backdrop, picking up the main hues from the pottery and hobnail Depression glass tumblers. A plaid ribbon wraps the votive holders.

Colorful floral napkins also link the dominant hues. If appropriate napkins can't be found, cotton fabric in a coordinating print can be purchased, cut into squares, and hemmed or serged to finish the edges.

WOVEN RIBBON MAT

Choose four pastel colors of acetate ribbon that coordinate with the vases and flowers being used. The mat can be created in a square, as on the table shown, or can be lengthened into a runner to fit other table shapes.

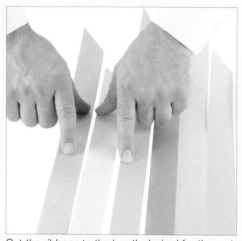

Cut the ribbons to the length desired for the mat, trimming the ends at an angle. Lay ribbons side by side, in an alternating pattern, until the proper width is achieved. Tape the top ends down temporarily, if desired.

Weave additional ribbons – alternating colors – into the vertical strips, alternately going over and under the strips. After the bottom is reached, loose tails should remain on all four sides. Remove any tape, if used.

RIBBON VOTIVES

Trim a length of plaid ribbon so that it encircles a glass votive cup, with the ends just meeting. Spray the cup with adhesive, and smooth on the ribbon.

Woven pastels pick up the soft hues of vintage pottery.

LUNCH ON THE LINKS

Score an ace with a golf-themed table perfect for celebrating Father's Day, honoring a golf enthusiast or relaxing after a round.

Two trays of pavéd carnations, button spray chrysanthemums, roses and 'Green Trick' *Dianthuses* – in a range of white, amber and green hues – are topped with an antique golf club and a single ball teed up in the floral foam. A low green tray filled with pea gravel calls to mind the waiting sand traps.

Snips of bear grass pressed between two clear plastic plates top dapper place mats cut from plaid wrapping paper. Decorative paper folded over and sealed with a tee holds the menu or other message for guests.

Clear plastic ornaments filled with all-white M&M candies, available for order or at craft stores, mimic golf balls and make delicious mementos.

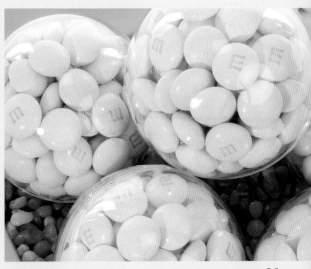

PAVÉD TRAYS

Paint a wood tray white. Cut a rectangle of plastic-coated foil, and press it into the tray, covering all the surfaces and cutting off any excess paper. This will keep water from leaking through the porous tray.

Cut blocks of soaked floral foam to fill the entire tray, shaving the pieces to just slightly below the tray's edge.

Cut flower stems short, and insert the flowers into the foam in tightly packed rows. Start at one end of the tray and work toward the other, alternating varieties to create an uninterrupted bed of pavéd florals.

GOLF-BALL MECHANICS

Golf balls make a quick, theme-specific armature to anchor a cluster of carnations in a decorative glass cube. Nestle the stems among the balls; no additional mechanics are needed.

Color, pattern and texture bring life to the table.

Diminutive nosegays surround an impressive floral "cake" on this simply elegant table set for a bridal shower or luncheon. The arrangements suggest the bouquets and confections to come at the wedding.

A profusion of roses, *Godetias*, asters and statice, ranging from delicate rose to hot pink hues, is accented with tufts of fluffy white baby's breath (*Gypsophila*). The layered salal leaf collar is crafted ahead of time rather than inserting the leaves one by one, as in the satellite arrangements. Gold-centered button blooms accessorize the individual arrangements, which are nestled into glass holders designed for pillar candles.

Elevating the flowers and keeping accessories minimal – rose-hued Depression glass and lace doilies – ensures the blooms are the focal point.

SALAL COLLAR

Gather groups of about three salal leaves into fan-shaped clusters, and staple the groups at the base of the leaves. Continue creating these clusters until there are enough to ring the cake stand.

To assemble the collar, staple individual clusters together at the bases, fanning the groupings slightly so that a complete circle sized to fit the cake stand eventually is achieved.

Staple the first and last clusters together to finish the ring, and lay the collar atop the cake stand. This method keeps the leaves in place and pointing the right directions without inserting each leaf individually.

STEMMING BUTTONS

Flower-shaped buttons are stemmed for insertion among the fresh blooms by placing a floral wire through the button loop, bending both ends downward and taping the wire with stem wrap.

Clear glass elevates and enhances the floral treats.

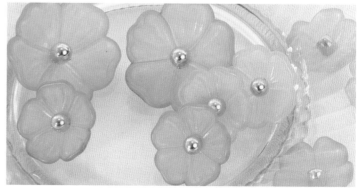

Ocean treasures await discovery on this fragrant, beach-themed table.

Beehive gingers (*Zingiber spectabile*), with their delightful aroma and distinctive shape, are tucked into a basket ringed with capiz shells. Orange and white *Freesias* slip into urchin-shaped bud glasses and bundled bamboo vases, alongside wispy Queen Anne's lace.

Amber hues with hints of blue reflect the sand and the sea. The gravel lining the center of the table, for a sandy base, is poured between two yardsticks to create the clean edges. Art glass starfish add interest, while candlesticks make unique pedestals for individual treasures, such as a single ginger and starfish.

Sea urchin shells threaded with twine bind the coral-patterned napkins along with a piece of bamboo, which can serve as a place marker.

BAMBOO VASES

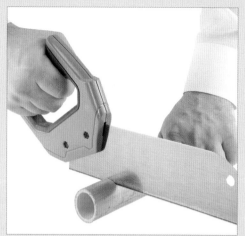

Cut bamboo into roughly equal lengths with a fine-toothed saw. Be sure a node (joint) is near the bottom of each section. Bamboo is hollow except for a membrane at the nodes, making the lengths into small, watertight vases.

Cluster a group of bamboo tubes, node sides down, and encircle the bundle with a rubber band. Water tubes can be inserted for extra insurance, if desired, or can be used if some of the lengths of bamboo don't have nodes.

Wrap twine around the bundle multiple times to cover the rubber band and enhance the nautical look, which resembles the pylons of a pier. Knot the ends of the twine when finished. Fill the tubes with flower-food solution.

REPURPOSED CANDLESTICKS

Matching stem wrap encircles the base of a beehive ginger, creating a fatter stem to secure it into a taper candleholder. On a starfish, the wrap smooths one of the points for insertion.

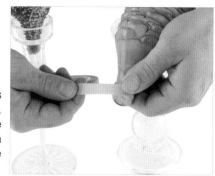

Glass candlesticks elevate singular seaside specimens.

ROSY RECEPTION

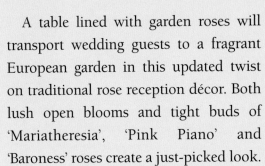

A table lined with garden roses will transport wedding guests to a fragrant European garden in this updated twist on traditional rose reception décor. Both lush open blooms and tight buds of 'Mariatheresia', 'Pink Piano' and 'Baroness' roses create a just-picked look.

Inexpensive clay long-tom pots and saucers become mossy, weather-aged accessories using a simple paint technique. The glass cloches, enjoying a resurgence, give a rare quality to the roses beneath and add to the candles' shimmer. Bits of reindeer moss hold the votives into their tiny pots.

Ivy-covered mats adorn each place setting, and gorgeous oversized images of the roses are printed, trimmed and placed beneath the clear glass plates. The art is available to download at *www.floristsreview.com/flowersforthetable*.

FAUX MOSS FINISH

Spray the surface of a terra-cotta pot heavily with water. The beaded water produces the uneven mottled effect. Then apply a light coat of Moss Green floral spray.

Immediately spray with more water. Follow with the next layer of color, Basil floral spray. Work around the entire pot. Again follow with a heavy spray of water.

Follow immediately with the third and last layer, Flat White floral spray. Finally, give the pot a last spritz of water. The finished effect, when dried, should be that of an aged, moss-covered pot.

IVY-LEAF PLACE MATS

Spray the backsides of individual ivy leaves with adhesive. Allow the adhesive to become tacky, then apply the leaves around the edges of a rectangular piece of kraft paper, creating a sawtooth (zigzag) pattern. Work toward the center.

Instant aging method adds intrigue to simple clay pots.

A rainbow of colors reflects a bounty of good wishes for an honored birthday guest at this festive table.

Colorful electrical tape is the secret ingredient that turns plain glass vases, candlesticks and drinking glasses into works of art to match the bold saturated hues of the *Gerberas*. Tape colors are alternated at random, and one can either mask an entire surface with stripes or strategically leave sections uncovered.

Art vases crafted of recycled magazines add a twist to the striped palette. Floating candles are a fun alternative to pillars in the stemmed candleholders. At both ends of the table, a *Gerbera* floats in a sequence of low trays.

Single blooms in votives resembling retro aluminum tumblers make fun party favors. And guests will get a kick out of eating off of "petal-covered" plates.

CUSTOM TAPING

Gather rolls of electrical tape in a variety of colors. Beginning at the base of a glass cylinder vase, wrap one of the tapes around the container. Cut the tape once it overlaps its starting point.

Wrap the next tape color around the vase, overlapping the first color slightly. Begin at the same starting/ending point so that any visible seam is in a single straight line, for a more polished look.

Continue alternating tape colors to cover the vase. Arrange a bundle of *Gerberas*, cut just taller than the vase, so that all heads face outward. Secure the grouping of flowers with waterproof tape before placing it into the vase.

PETAL-PERFECT PLATES

Pluck *Gerbera* petals in a variety of colors. Lay them randomly onto a clear plastic plate, and place a second plate atop so that the petals are sandwiched in between.

Creative color combinations are sure to bring smiles.

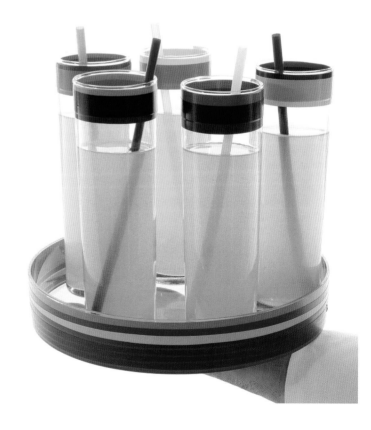

A trio of delightful doggies greet guests preparing to welcome a new bundle of joy. The pink, lime and chocolate brown palette will appeal to mom whether she is expecting a girl or a boy.

Football and cushion spray chrysanthemums dyed pink are wired together for the pups' heads and arranged into a bed of more mums and salal leaves in a fabric-lined basket. To prepare the basket to accommodate water-soaked floral foam, line it with plastic-coated foil. 'Sweet Sensation' spray roses are laid casually into glass cylinder vases wrapped in ribbon. Spray adhesive holds the two wide ribbons in place, and an adhesive dot secures the bow.

Seek out coordinating items from a variety of sources, such as the pastel dog bowls – found at a pet shop – that each display a single football mum. Floral note cards become place cards, and a colorful stuffed cow is a sweet gift for baby.

PINK POODLES

For the pup's face, wire a football mum, and gently bend the stem so that the bloom faces forward. Bundle this mum just underneath an upright mum and back to back with another bent-stemmed mum. Bind the trio of stems with waterproof tape.

To create each of the pup's ears, thread five or six cushion spray mums onto a thin-gauge wire. Form a hook at the end of the wire to secure the mums. Tape a heavier-gauge wire to the other end of the thinner wire with stem wrap.

Bend the wire on each ear so that the cushion mums face downward. Place one ear on each side of the football mum grouping, and tape the wire stems to the stem bundle with waterproof tape. Glue on the eyes, craft-foam tongue, nose (a plastic grape painted black) and ribbons with liquid floral adhesive.

DYE JOBS

The pink chrysanthemums are colored with floral dip dye, available at flower shops and craft stores. Dip white mums into the dye, shake off the excess and rinse the blooms in clear water. Let the flowers dry before using.

Floral dye matches mums to the soft pink rose hue.

JAPANESE GARDEN

The clever repurposing of carnation stems to create a bamboo effect helps reinforce the theme in this vivid garden table, set for sushi, sashimi or other Asian fare.

Custom tableware is created by applying calendar art to the undersides of clear glass salad plates. Later, the images can be soaked off and the plates reused.

The "bamboo" – which cages striking groups of spider chrysanthemums, callas, carnations, *Hypericum* and *Camellia* leaves – is actually leftover carnations stems that have been stripped of their leaves, with a few red twig dogwood stems mixed in.

Touches of color abound. *Hypericum* berries float in the jewel-like chopstick bowls and alongside *Camellia* leaves in the clear finger bowls. A cobalt ikebana vase at each end of the table holds a single purple fuji chrysanthemum.

"BAMBOO" HEDGES

Cut a block of floral foam sized to extend several inches above the rim of the rectangular ceramic container, leaving about a ½-inch-wide reservoir on each side. Secure the foam into the container with hot-melt (pan) glue.

Cut narrow pieces of floral foam to rest flush with the rim of the container and fill in the spaces between the main block of foam and the container edges. Press these foam pieces into the container.

Strip the leaves from leftover carnation stems, and cut the stems to equal lengths. Insert the stems into the foam, around the edge of the container, to create a screen effect. Intersperse a few stems of red twig dogwood. Arrange flowers into the center.

DECOUPAGE PLATES

Soak an image in a mixture of water and white glue, and smooth the paper onto the underside of a clear salad plate. A second plate can be pressed against the paper to help it conform, then removed. Trim away the excess paper when it's dry.

Japanese art, faux bamboo and red hues set the mood.

SWEET SOCIAL

Whether celebrating a Sweet 16 or other special birthday, a young girl will find her heart's desire reflected in this delectable all-pink collection. Colorful candies and carnation petals fill apothecary jars, two of which are based with lush wreaths of burgundy to blush carnations, the varied hues adding interest.

Butterflies crafted of beads and metallic wire swirl above. A small wire is bent into a V and inserted into the top of each bead to form the antenna. One butterfly is pushed onto each end of a length of wire, and the center of the wire is wrapped around the finial atop the jar lid.

Rectangles of dark and light pink craft foam alternate down the length of the table, creating an inexpensive runner, and bead butterflies glued to glittery corsage bracelets serve as bejeweled napkin rings.

CARNATION RINGS

For the carnation wreaths, use floral-foam wreath forms in plastic trays. The center should be large enough to accommodate the base of a large apothecary jar. Pour flower-food solution into the tray's center to saturate the foam.

Place the candy-filled apothecary jar into the center of the wreath form after all the solution has been absorbed. Placing the jar before the carnations allows the flowers to completely surround the jar's base.

Cut the carnation stems short, and insert them into the wreath form, creating a mounded shape that completely covers the floral foam. Arrange the carnations so that the various hues are sprinkled throughout the wreath.

PETAL-FILLED URNS

Snip the carnation petals just above the green calyx. This not only is faster but also eliminates the green portion that remains when petals are plucked by hand.

Solid and bicolor blooms spice up a sweet palette.

VEGGIE DELIGHT

Fresh produce joins florals on a summery garden table.

Choose a variety of colorful vegetables to display, either on their own or nestled into small clay pots. Asparagus and carrots make organic vessels – hiding water tubes and a clay pot, respectively – for the flowers. Make these the day of the event to keep them fresh. A rainbow of colorful *Gerberas*, carnations, 'Green Trick' *Dianthuses*, *Hydrangeas* and *Hypericum* complements the produce.

Inexpensive clay pots and saucers serve as everything from coasters and plates to napkin rings. The napkin rings are created by chipping off the bottom of a miniature clay pot with a craft knife and then filing the base smooth. Plaid linen is then threaded through.

Beautiful old-fashioned seed packets dress up the table and give guests their own garden start.

63

CARROT POT

Secure a clay pot into a clay saucer, at least one size larger, using hot-melt (pan) glue. Line the pot with plastic-coated foil before adding floral foam.

Wrap a rubber band around the pot. Cut carrots to equal lengths, just taller than the pot rim. Dip the carrot tips into liquid floral adhesive, and insert the carrots behind the rubber band and into the saucer, encircling the pot.

Pack reindeer moss into the saucer around the carrots. This will help anchor the vegetables and add a pleasing finishing touch. Tie raffia around the carrots to cover the rubber-band binding.

ASPARAGUS VASES

Place a glass or plastic water tube into the center of a foam-filled clay pot. Insert equal lengths of asparagus into the foam, completely surrounding the tube. Bind the bundle with waterproof tape, and cover the tape with raffia.

Veggies make inexpensive décor for a summer table.

64

Monobotanical arrangements make it a cinch to festoon a table with an explosion of red, white and blue for an Independence Day party.

Vintage-looking striped fabric encircles cylinder vases holding 'Alabaster' garden roses, *Hydrangeas*, carnations, *Hypericum* and *Delphiniums*. A few red and blue glass saucers reinforce the color scheme.

Adding to the old-time charm are a patriotic crocheted potholder, Nantucket baskets – one holding a vintage hanky – and a boater hat wrapped in ribbon. The same ribbon is applied in a single strip with spray adhesive to tall red cylinder vases, resembling firecrackers. The floral fan is crafted from an old advertising placard.

Delft china repeats the brilliant blue of the *Delphiniums* and adds an upscale touch to the patriotic ensemble.

FABRIC-WRAP VASES

Cut a piece of fabric wide enough to encircle a cylinder vase. Make it the height of the vase plus about 1½ inches. Apply double-face tape to the front side of the fabric, flush with the edge.

Fold over the taped strip of fabric, creating a "cuff" the width of the tape. Apply another strip of tape in the same manner, and fold it over again, to create finished edges on the top and bottom of the cuff.

Apply a strip of double-face tape vertically onto the vase. Apply one end of the fabric to the tape, with the cuff at the bottom, and wrap the fabric tightly around the vase. Adhere the loose end of the fabric with another strip of double-face tape.

PETALED FANS

A promotional fan gets a fanciful update with a covering of *Hydrangea* blossoms, which are applied with spray adhesive. Work from the outside edges of the fan toward the center.

Coordinating stripes boldly display patriotic panache.

Transport guests to the tropics with a table inspired by pink ginger and colorful elephant's-ear (*Caladium*) leaves.

Everyday blooms and foliage – bicolor carnations, *Alstroemerias*, 'Pink Piano' roses, *Hypericum* and salal leaves – take on an island feel when arranged into coconut husk containers and bamboo vases. The coconut husk, commonly used in hanging baskets, is made waterproof with plastic liners.

The *Caladium* leaf mat is crafted of three varieties of leaves, which are applied to a large square of kraft paper with spray adhesive. Once the desired flowerlike shape is achieved, trim around the leaves, and spray with a sealant to prevent the leaves from drying out.

Carnation leis and parlor-palm "trees" add to the ambience along with the coconut accents and bold napkins.

PARLOR-PALM TREES

Cut a handful of stems from a parlor palm (*Chamaedorea*), and assemble them into a bunch.

Insert a hyacinth stake into the center of the palm bundle, and bind the stems together with stem wrap. Tape the entire length of the stake.

Wrap the "stem" with sheer pink ribbon. Start at the top, leaving a bit of tail to tie off at the end, and wrap to the bottom and back up again. Tie off the end of the ribbon to the initial tail.

CARNATION LEIS

Cut off carnation stems just below the calyxes. Using an upholstery needle and string, sew through the blooms' centers, one after another, pushing them close together to form a lei.

Everyday flowers and leaves take on a tropical twist.

A flutter of feather butterflies (*mariposas*) alights on this vibrant table set for a fiesta celebration. The monarch butterfly, known for its annual migration and vivid coloration, is a perfect choice.

The butterflies are on thin wires, and their placement, both individually and in mass, enhances their realism. One even appears to float in midair.

Monobotanical arrangements of *Alstroemerias*, 'Sunset' roses, baby's breath (*Gypsophila*) and 'Granny Smith' apples complement the hues in the Spanish-style patterns on the plates and napkins. A mix of simple white pottery contains the arrangements and lets the flowers take center stage.

Several of the apples are transformed into bud vases with the addition of water tubes, and salal leaves add the fruit's greenery.

CORED-APPLE VASES

Core a hole into the center of an apple. If desired, spritz inside with lemon juice or Fruit-Fresh Produce Protector to delay the browning process.

Insert a glass or plastic water tube into the hole. Fill it with flower-food solution, and insert one or several blooms.

To create the apple leaf, choose a smaller salal leaf, and pierce its base with a hairpin wire. Twist one side of the hairpin around the other, creating a single insertion point to pierce into the center of the apple.

BUTTERFLY POSITIONING

The wired feather butterflies are simply inserted into the mass of baby's breath. A dollop of floral adhesive at the end of the wire secures each among the florets.

The monarch's bold colors complement a fiesta theme.

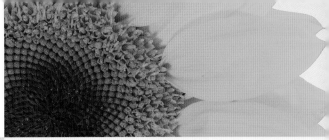

Add sunny punch to a summer barbecue or casual gathering with a spread of sunflowers and *Hydrangeas* surrounded by denim and straw.

Recycled jeans – from the back of the closet or a thrift store – encircle cornflower-colored *Hydrangeas* and two varieties of sunflowers in a trio of arrangements interspersed with sunflower-filled straw bales. The pockets from the jeans hold the silverware and napkins. Even smaller straw bales, available from floral and craft suppliers, prop up the place cards.

Mason jars serve as individual jugs for enjoying sweet tea or lemonade, and horse-themed plates, in a matching blue hue, await the country fare. Biodegradable bamboo chargers add a formal touch while keeping with the natural, eco-friendly aspects of the setting.

DENIM CONTAINERS

Cut the legs from a pair of old or inexpensive blue jeans. Cut parallel to the cuff at a length just taller than the vase to be covered. (Set the pockets aside to be cut out for the napkin holders.)

Apply double-sided adhesive strips around the outer rim of the glass vase. Remove the paper backing to expose the adhesive.

Slip the jeans leg over the vase, with the hem at the bottom. Roll under the unfinished edge, and press the fabric to the adhesive, creating a quick tailored edge that won't wick any water from the vase.

HAY-BALE VASES

Set a mini straw bale on end. Using a craft knife, carve a hole just large enough to accommodate a water tube into the end of the bale. Insert a sunflower-filled water tube.

Repurposed jeans create cool, casual accessories.

WINE TASTING

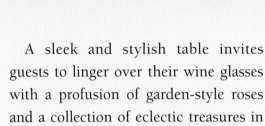

A sleek and stylish table invites guests to linger over their wine glasses with a profusion of garden-style roses and a collection of eclectic treasures in vintage printer's box table runners.

The brilliant blooms and colorful geodes, *Hypericum* berries, shells and mosses among the boxes' sections contrast the blacks and browns that predominate. An antique basket and willow-trunk topiaries hold 'Fiction', 'Piano', 'Freee' (yes, it has three "e"s), 'Wanted', 'Baroness', 'Mariatheresia' and 'Caramel Antike' roses. *Heuchera* (coralbells) leaves accent the floral mounds. Dainty glass bud vases bring a few blooms down to the table.

Topiaries are a great choice for parties where guests will be both sitting and standing, adding height to the setting while not impeding the view.

WILLOW TOPIARIES

Cut willow branches (*Salix*) to even lengths, and insert the willows into the opening of an urn. Continue adding branches to completely fill the urn, which will keeping the willows standing upright.

Tape a thin-gauge wire with brown stem wrap to match the hue of the willow branches. Encircle the top of the branch bundle with the wire, which will keep the willows tightly compacted and help support the flowers.

Insert a foam-filled bouquet holder that has been soaked in flower-food solution into the center of the willow bundle. Arrange roses into the foam.

PRINTER'S BOX

Vintage or reproduction printer's boxes can be used to create dramatic table runners when filled with varied bits of this and that. Here, an aggregation of botanicals, minerals and other elements of nature are intermingled with wine bottle corks, which establish the theme of this party.

Topiaries add height but won't block guests' view.

Whether celebrating the Friday night lights or a weekend on the gridiron, fans will find lots to cheer at this upscale tailgate party.

The amber beer bottles do triple-duty, serving as tall bud vases for the clustering of birds-of-paradise; as smaller vases for monobotanical bunches of *Hydrangeas*, carnations and 'Orange Unique' roses; and as votive candleholders. A bottle-cutting kit creates the clean breaks for these one-of-a-kind accents.

Orange and blue craft foam pennants appear to wave in the wind, and the same foam serves as place mats. A field of turflike green fabric anchors the centerpiece.

The birds-of-paradise, in particular, are chosen for their blue-and-orange coloring, but this look can be customized to any team's colors by seeking suitable blooms.

FOAM PENNANTS

Select sheets of craft foam in the team colors. Holding the sheets together, cut out a triangular pennant shape.

Bend a floral wire into a V shape, and sandwich it between the two foam triangles, using spray adhesive to affix the wire and hold the triangles together. Trim the wire so that it doesn't extend past the edges of the foam.

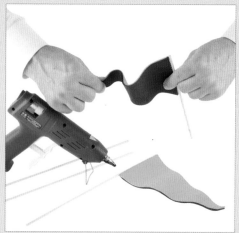

Secure a wooden skewer to the pennant with hot glue. Bend and smooth the wire-centered foam into a wavelike shape, suggesting the pennant is blowing in the breeze. The wire allows it to maintain this shape.

BOTTLE CUTTING

Beer bottles become ideal vases and votive holders. A bottle-cutting kit scores the glass, and heat and cold separate it. We used Ephrem's Bottle Cutter, *www.delphiglass.com*.

Recycled bottles make great vases and votives.

SPOOKY SUPPER

The addition of purple adds intrigue to the iconic Halloween pairing of orange and black while expanding the palette of fright-worthy florals.

Translucent spider webs – cleverly crafted from hot glue – shimmer on painted funeral baskets in this spooky setting while twisted bare branches add an ominous touch to the arrangements of *Alstroemerias*, carnations, *Gerberas*, New York *Asters* and lamb's-ears (*Stachys*) foliage. Violet-hued 'Moonlite' carnations are featured in the rusted metal vase at the table's center.

An iron cat keeps watch, and batlike devil's claw (*Proboscidea*) pods add interest among the blooms and on the table. Pumpkins are placed generously around the table, and the addition of a black mask creates a quick whimsical take on the traditional jack-o'-lantern.

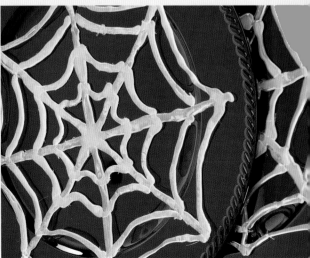

HOT-GLUE COBWEBS

Spray a glass tray thoroughly with lubricant, such as leaf-shine spray or cooking spray. Any size pan can be used; a 12-inch-square glass tray is shown here.

Using a hot glue gun, draw two lines, from corner to corner of the tray, to create an X. Draw two more lines, from side to side of the tray, to create a second X bisecting the first.

Draw concave loops from line to line in a concentric pattern. Immediately harden the web by running cool water over it, and peel it off the glass. If left too long, it will be tough to remove. Glue the webs to the basket handles.

BASKET BLACKING

Paint old-fashioned funeral baskets with Flat Black floral spray so that they match each other and the Halloween palette.

Translucent spider webs add a spooky shimmer.

NATURE'S BOUNTY

Textural orbs and shocks of copper-bound barley displayed in a wood gathering bowl draw attention amid the surrounding neutral blonde hues of this fall table.

Carnation and *Hypericum* spheres provide pops of color, and the barley is the ideal harvest icon. Experiment with creating spheres from other floral materials, or purchase premade orbs of wood, seeds or other natural elements.

Sisal mesh creates the table runner. A small flock of carved wood birds alight among the carnations and upon tiny perches. Decorative painted gourds and leaf ornaments are additional reminders of the natural world.

The creamy candles sit on natural wood coasters, and biodegradable bamboo chargers set off the place settings. Dried gourds in parfait glasses add the finishing touch.

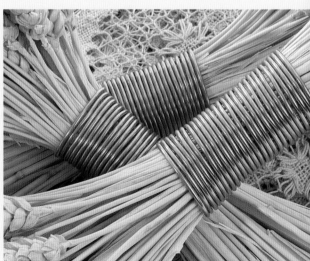

CARNATION ORBS

Soak a floral-foam sphere in properly mixed flower-food solution. Place the sphere onto a pedestal candleholder to keep it elevated and steady, making it easier to work with hands-free. A tray below will catch any drips.

Cut the carnation stems with a sharp knife, leaving about a half-inch of stem to insert into the foam. Be sure to cut the stems at an angle so that the pointed stem ends can be inserted easily and cleanly into the floral-foam sphere.

Dip the carnation stems into liquid floral adhesive, and push them firmly into the floral foam. Place the flowers close together, and work around the sphere, covering it completely.

BARLEY SHEAVES

Gather a bundle of barley, turning it over so that the heads fall to the same level and any loose bits drop out. Wrap the bundle with waterproof tape and then with decorative wire.

A neutral backdrop sets off a banquet of fall textures.

Bold blooms celebrate the abundance of Thanksgiving on a table that combines interesting organic containers with a gathering of vintage and new tableware.

The eclectic collection of Depression glass, reproduction Majolica plates and family heirlooms inspires the *Galax*-covered pots of *Gerberas*, spray chrysanthemums, *Ranunculi*, miniature callas, sea holly (*Eryngium*) and *Hypericum*. The "twigs" are actually the stems of the *Galax* leaves.

Many ingredients for this table can be found at the grocery store. Naturally vivid cauliflower varieties nestle into herb-covered cornucopias. Artichokes reinforce the muted green of the plates, and a hollowed gourd is transformed into a rustic basket of purple button spray mums.

Plaid linens reflect even more of the flower colors on the tabletop.

PARSLEY HORNS

Spray a grapevine cornucopia with adhesive. Allow time for the adhesive to become tacky – 45 to 60 seconds. Apply a second coating of adhesive just before covering with parsley.

Sprinkle dried parsley flakes onto the adhesive-coated cornucopia. Work in small sections to minimize fall off of the parsley flakes.

Pat the parsley flakes so that they adhere firmly to the cornucopia and completely cover it. Fill in bare areas by spraying them with additional adhesive and sprinkling on more parsley flakes.

GALAX-LEAF POTS

Spray the backsides of *Galax* leaves with adhesive, and press them, stems up, around the rim of a clay pot. Continue down the pot, removing the stems as you near the base.

Galax stems add height and movement among blooms.

A rich red tartan inspires this abundant display of red and purple blooms complemented by red glass and silver accents. Striking *Eryngium* (sea holly) blooms call to mind Scotland's national flower, the thistle.

A footed pewter soup tureen holds the lavish grouping of 'Latin Lady' and 'Red Bentley' roses along with *Freesias*, *Eryngiums* and *Hypericum*. The same blooms ring the base in a floral-foam wreath form on the pewter tray.

Like cranberries threaded for the holidays, a strand of *Hypericum* berries is gracefully looped around the tureen. Instead of foliage, metallic wire leaves add sparkle when incorporated, in trios, into the main arrangement. They also accessorize single *Eryngium* blooms tucked into the silver napkin holders.

METAL LEAVES

Form a loop at the end of a length of silver metallic wire. Holding the wire with needle-nose pliers, twist the loop to secure it.

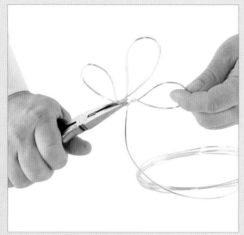

Form two more similarly sized loops, in succession, after the first, twisting off the loops as they are created.

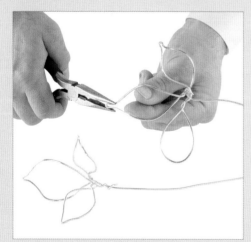

Crimp the top of each loop into a point with the needle-nose pliers to create a leaf shape. It may be necessary to crimp the end and then open it back up a bit with the pliers so that the point is more natural and less severe.

BERRY GARLANDS

String *Hypericum* berries onto thin beading wire to create the garland. One long strand is used in the main arrangement, with the looped portions held in place by wood picks.

Tartan inspires new colors and forms for the holiday.

Glittering oversized jewels and gold and silver accents add elegance to a gathering of natural elements, marking the winter solstice and the longer nights to come.

The centerpiece is a natural wood tray filled with an orb of 'Eskimo' roses, bundles of lamb's-ears (*Stachys*) foliage in water tubes, wax-coated pine cones and nests, and crackle glass ornaments. Button spray chrysanthemums at each place setting are nestled into votive-size mint julep cups. A bundle of pheasant feathers is bound with metallic wire, and lamb's-ears create a living wreath.

Sheets of Italian wrapping paper cut into place mats give the illusion of an animal print from afar. For the napkins, linen is trimmed to size, and a few threads are pulled from each side to create the frayed edges.

WAX SURFACING

Remove the wick from a white pillar candle, and set it into a large glue skillet or an electric skillet dedicated to wax melting. Melt the wax. It is ready to use when it is just barely white on the surface.

Wrap one end of a straight floral wire around a large pine cone, between two rows of scales, to create a handle for suspending the cone. The handle also can be used to dip the cone into the wax, if that method is preferred.

Hold the pine cone over the skillet, and spoon wax over the cone. It should solidify almost immediately. Repeat until the desired coating is achieved. If preferred, dip the cone directly into the wax.

LEAF-COVERED WREATH

Spray the backs of lamb's-ears leaves with adhesive, and apply them to a plastic-foam wreath form – overlapping first in one direction and then the opposite – to cover it.

Natural "found art" items dress up a solstice table.

A fresh take on the classic red-and-white Christmas pairing makes for an inviting table. Picot-edged bicolor carnations stand out among the all-red carnations and 'Red Bentley' roses, white *Hydrangeas,* and *Heuchera* (coral-bells) foliage tucked into cozy knit-covered vases and a mint-julep-style vessel.

Red-glass ornaments in silver-painted pots create unique bud vases. Sparkling silver bells are wired into the arrangements, and smaller versions are gathered in glittering groupings in the parfait cups. Glossy pillar candles on glass pedestals add height and warmth to the table.

Silver-painted clothespins hold place cards featuring a vintage Saint Nick, the perfect complement to the candy-striped place mats cut from Italian wrapping paper.

CABLE-KNIT COVER

Cut off the end of a knitted sock, keeping the cuff intact and leaving enough length to extend about a half-inch past the base of a small cylinder vase. Slip the sock over the vase. The turned-down edge gives a cozy finish.

Turn the vase over. Secure the raw edge of the sock onto the base of the glass using a hot-glue gun. A small knife can help press down the edge and avoid burning fingers in the hot glue.

Cut a circle of red felt slightly smaller than the bottom of the vase. Apply hot-glue just inside the edge of the base, and press down the felt. This gives a smooth foundation and keeps the knit from unraveling or slipping.

ORNAMENT CONTAINER

Remove the cap and hanger from a kugel or other round glass ornament. Set, or glue, the ornament into a silver-painted clay pot. Insert flowers into the ornament's opening.

Cable knits and candy-cane colors evoke holiday cheer.

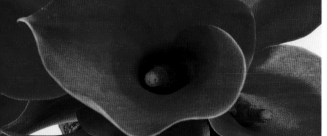

The drama of the New Year's Eve countdown is matched by the stunning fuchsia-colored blooms on an all-black table with gilded accents.

Traditional urns make classy topiaries ringed with bicolor carnations and bursting with 'Yves Piaget' garden roses, carnations, *Heuchera* (coral-bells) leaves and golden pomegranates. The low arrangement extends the look with graceful callas. 'Frangancia' roses are massed in golden pots, and gilded wire cloches add style.

Gilt picture frames are used as bases for the urn topiaries, repeating the gold of the fruit. Flocked paper in a rich purple is cut into tactile place mats.

If needed, flat black paint can unite decorative items in the midnight palette, such as the tray, miniature urns holding cocktail skewers, and towering candlesticks.

CARNATION COLLAR

Carve a block of floral foam into a roughly cylindrical shape to fit into an urn. Stand the block on end, and slice off edges until the right size is achieved. Square corners make it difficult to create a rounded arrangement.

Dip one end of the carved column of floral-foam into hot-melt (pan) glue, and place the foam into the urn. Fill the urn with flower-food solution, and allow the foam to absorb it. Continue to add flower-food solution until the foam is thoroughly saturated.

Arrange carnations, with their stems cut short, into the foam in a horizontal fashion. Encircle the foam, and extend up a few rows to create a wide collar of carnations. Arrange the other ingredients above this collar.

GILDED POMEGRANATE

Pierce a hole into the bottom of each dried pomegranate, and glue a wood pick into each hole with hot glue. Paint each pomegranate with Brilliant Gold floral spray.

Gilt accents add shimmer to the dramatic setting.

FLORISTS' REVIEW

FLOWERS FOR THE TABLE

President of Florists' Review Enterprises: Frances Dudley, AAF
Publisher and Floral Designer: Talmage McLaurin, AIFD
Author: Amy Bauer
Photographer and Art Director: John Collins
Creative Coordinator: James Miller, AIFD
Copy Editor: Amy Bauer and David Coake

© 2010, Florists' Review Enterprises, Inc.

All Rights Reserved.
No part of this publication may be reproduced without prior written permission from the publisher.

Florists' Review Flowers for the Table
was produced by Florists' Review Enterprises, Inc.,
Topeka, Kansas; *www.floristsreview.com.*

Printed in China by
Regent Publishing Services Ltd.
Shau Kei Wan, Hong Kong

ISBN: 978-0-9801815-5-5

Florists' Review Enterprises is the leading magazine and book publishing company for the U.S. floral industry. The company is home to *Florists' Review* and *Super Floral Retailing* magazines as well as to Florists' Review Bookstore, the industry's premier marketplace for books and other educational materials.

A special thanks to Alexandra Farms and Esmeralda Farms for their generous support.

For other titles from *Florists' Review*, visit our website,
www.floristsreview.com

The flowers in this book were provided by Asocolflores-member farms in Colombia;
all were sustainably grown and Florverde® certified.